LIVING IN THE

Last Days

LIVING IN THE
Last Days

DARRYL JOHNSON

XULON PRESS

Xulon Press
2301 Lucien Way #415
Maitland, FL 32751
407.339.4217
www.xulonpress.com

Printed in the United States of America.

ISBN-13: 978-1-5456-7186-3

By listening to the headlines discussed
on nearly all of your news networks,
you don't have to be a bible scholar
to know that we are living in the days that
were prophesied by the Old Testment Prophets,
spoken of by the Disciples of Jesus,
and proclaimed

TABLE OF CONTENTS

FORWARD

Truly, this is a Son of God, Darryl Johnson, I met Darryl in 1987, he has a beautiful wife and family. This couple are the one's who opened the door in 1989 to tell my revelation in Fort Washington Maryland, which then went all over the world. Many doors of God opened for me after I met this family of God. This young man of God will open the eyes of many concerning End Time Events!! He has been through the fire and storms of life and I believe in him. I pray that the Glory of God be with this book and that goes around the world and change many lives as mine did.

Dr. Mary K. Baxter

LIVING IN THE LAST DAYS

But, beloved, be not ignorant of this one thing, that one day is with the Lord as a thousand years, and a thousand years as one day. The Lord is not slack concerning his promise, as some men count slackness; but is longsuffering to us-ward, not willing that any should perish, but that all should come to repentance. But the day of the Lord will come as a thief in the night; in which the heavens shall pass away with a great noise, and the elements shall melt with fervent heat, the earth also and the works that are therein shall be burned up.

Seeing then that all these things shall be dissolved, what manner of persons ought ye to be in all holy conversation and godliness. Looking for and hasting unto the coming of the day of God, wherein the heavens being on fire shall be dissolved, and the elements shall melt with fervent heat? [2 Pet. 3:8-12]

The phrase "living in the last days" has been used for nearly two thousand years to describe the period of time when specific prophecies regarding the end of days would occur and to predict the timing of certain events to take place that are spoken of in both the Old and New Testaments in the Holy Bible. I concur that if you had the ability to sit down with many of our Bible scholars and religious leaders that have followed these trends over the last few decades, there would be broad agreement that the pattern of events that we are witnessing today are signs that we truly are living in the last days.

Turning on the evening news or picking up a newspaper anywhere in the world will confirm that signs the Bible spoke of concerning the end of days are not only true but are accelerating at breathtaking speed. In the gospel of Matthew, Jesus Christ predicted that right before His second appearing, certain signs would occur that would prove how close His return really was. He also gave an admonishing word that when we, the Church, begin to see these things, we are to rejoice and be exceedingly glad.

I personally believe that what we are witnessing today, with respect to terrorism, financial instability, lawlessness, soaring worldwide crime, moral corruption, and decay, along with the threat of global warming, all points to the fact that not only has the beginning of the end started, but we are actually experiencing the birth pains of things to come. The Bible clearly warns that as we move closer toward the second coming of Jesus Christ, world conditions won't get better but much worse. In the gospel of Matthew, Jesus said that if it were not for the very elect's sake, no flesh would be saved, indicating that a time of great distress and worldwide suffering would climax to such a point that the world wouldn't be able to endure it, and total annihilation of mankind and the destruction of the planet would all be certain.

Jesus warned in the gospel of Luke that there would be a generation alive that would see certain signs that could be used to measure the nearness of His reappearance. These signs would prove that His coming was eminent. Jesus predicted that

- Nations (ethnic groups) would rise against nations
- Kingdoms would rise against kingdoms
- Famines and earthquakes would be in diverse places
- There would be suffering on a worldwide scale
- Pestilences and incurable deceases would spread
- Violence would be the norm of the day in many nations
- False Christ and false prophets would arise to deceive many

All of this was just the start of what Jesus said would be the "beginning of sorrows." The dishonor of the Word of God in our present generation is the root cause as to why many in our society no longer respect God or His son. As believers in Christ, we must be careful to not only preach the true gospel of Jesus Christ but to live it, because those that don't know the Lord are watching, and they aren't really interested too much in what we say but how we live.

The Bible also warns that in the last days there will be a great falling away from the truth [2 Thess. 2:23 KJV]. Sadly, what we are seeing today in some church circles is shocking. Some who at one time believed that the entire Word of God was inspired are now challenging many doctrinal beliefs that were once held up as sound doctrine without compromise. What was once considered biblical reality is now being replaced with political correctness for the sake of unity and love.

The Bible warns that a time would come that many would not be able to hear or accept sound doctrine, but would seek out teachers that only taught things that agreed with their lifestyles and their carnal understanding. ["For the time will come when they will not endure sound doctrine; but after their own lust shall they heap to themselves teachers, having itching ears; and they shall turn their ears from the truth, and shall be turned into fables" 2 Tim. 4:3-4 KJV]. Notice that the turning away would be a deliberate choice.

We must not forget that the same God who warned Noah of a flood that would come to destroy mankind from the face of the earth in the book of Genesis is the same God that has warned us of coming destruction in our day. We will continue on the current downward spiral toward becoming a society that not only disrespects the holiness of God but ignores His warnings. The same God that brought destruction by a global flood in Noah's day will bring destruction by fire the next time, which could be in the very near future.

Just as it was when Jesus came the first time nearly two thousand years ago and the people of His day failed to see the hour in which they were living and missed what the Bible describes in the book of Luke as their day of visitation, many in our present generation are also failing to recognize the signs of the times. As Israel of old, they are in jeopardy of not only missing out on what the Lord is doing in this time of the end but also the coming of the Lord Jesus all altogether, in what the Bible describes as the catching away.

> For the days shall come upon thee, that thine enemies shall cast a trench about thee, and compass thee round, and keep thee in on every side, and

shall lay thee even with the ground, and thy children within thee; and they shall not leave in thee one stone upon another; because thou knewest not the time of thy visitation. [Luke 19:43-44 KJV]

This lack of discernment has been the culprit of some in the Church spiritually falling asleep and no longer having that zeal for God that they once had. In some circles, there's even talk that those who teach on the coming of the Lord are teaching what is called escapism. This type of thinking is completely opposite of what the Bible teaches. Jesus warned that when He returns, He would suddenly appear to those that were *looking for him*. "So Christ was once offered to bear the sins of many; and unto them that look for him shall he appear the second time without sin unto salvation" [Heb. 9:28].

The phrase "looking for him" implies a sense of watching with great anticipation and expectation or eagerness. According to the gospel of John, those who live their lives with this type of mindset are purifying themselves, even as the Lord their God is pure.

[Behold what manner of love the Father hath bestowed upon us, that we should be called the sons of God: therefore the world knoweth us not, because it knew him not. Beloved, now are we the sons of God, and it doth not yet appear what we shall be: but we know that when he shall appear, we shall be like him: for we shall see him as he is. And every man that hath this hope in himself purifieth himself, even as he is pure. 1 John 3:1-3 KJV]

The doctrine of the coming of the Lord should never be given to spark fear but preparation and excitement as we near the end of this present dispensation and look with joy to the ages to come in the presence of the Lord Jesus Christ. However, there is still much more to be done and a very short time to do it before Jesus returns. This is the time for the believers in Christ to fulfill their righteous obligation the Lord Jesus Christ Himself has given them—to reach out to a lost and dying world with every tool possible. During His ministry, Jesus rebuked the religious leaders of His day because they didn't accurately discern the signs of the times. Matthew records it as follows:

> Now the Pharisees and Sadducees came up to Jesus, and they asked Him to show them a sign (spectacular miracle) from heaven (attesting His divine authority). He replied to them, when it is evening you say, it will be fair weather, for the sky is red, and in the morning, it will be stormy today, for the sky is red and has a gloomy and threatening look. You know how to interpret the appearance of the sky, but you cannot interpret the signs of the times. [Matt. 16:1-3 AMP]

Jesus has given the Church nearly two thousand years to take His message of salvation and healing to the world, and the Church has been and is presently doing this worldwide by the way of television, radio, missionaries, and personal evangelism. Great progress is being made all over the world in spreading the gospel of Jesus Christ, especially now in the Middle East and third world nations; the gospel is also starting to flourish among many Muslim nations. I personally believe that since the Iraqi invasion in 2001 by the United States and its allies, there seems to be a new openness toward the gospel in that part of the world.

We must remember that our time to work for Christ is coming to an end, and what we do for Christ, *we must do quickly.* I believe that God raised up the gentile Church within America to take His Word to the nations of the world. I also believe that if America forsakes that call and purpose, our country will lose its influence around the world as one of the greatest nations on the face of the planet. Unfortunately, just like the Roman Empire, who wasn't destroyed from without but from within, America is headed in this direction.

So it's truly time to embrace the signs that the Lord is allowing us to see and to use them as a witnessing tool to convince others of how close we are to the return of the Lord. People seem to be more open to hearing about the things of God during a crisis or a hard time than they are when things are going well. We seem to see our real need for God when we are at our lowest point.

After the terror attacks of 911, global terror warnings and even the talk of nuclear war have caused people to ask questions about where we are headed as a society. This is the time for the believers in Christ to reach others with the gospel of Christ because the number of unsaved people in the world is truly vast, and the Lord is not willing that any perish.

The signs of the coming of the Lord are all around us, and the hour of His appearing is getting closer day by day. For believers who are walking with God and are ready, this is a reason to rejoice and be exceedingly glad.

THE DAYS OF NOAH

*I*magine what Noah had to deal with in his generation after God had told him that He was about to send a global flood upon the entire face of the earth that would destroy every living person except for him and his family.

> "And God said to Noah, The end of all flesh is come before me; for the earth is filled with violence through them; and, behold, I will destroy them with the earth" [Gen. 6:13].

Not only did Noah have to convince himself that what God had told him would really come to pass, but his family members had to be convinced also. I'm sure that they had many questions as they proceeded with the task of building this huge boat. From the day God created the earth until then, it had never rained before; this was the very first time anything of that magnitude had ever happened.

The Bible is clear that Noah did his very best to warn his generation of the coming destruction; according to the Word of God, he was vexed with the blatant, outright disrespect for moral decency, and this grieved him daily. In that time, sin had become so horrible that God Himself was actually grieved within His own heart that He had ever created mankind.

> And God saw that the wickedness of man was great in the earth, and that every imagination of the thoughts of his heart was only evil continually. And it repented the Lord that he had made man on the earth, and it grieved him at his heart. And the Lord said, I will destroy man whom I have created from the face of the earth; both man, and beast, and the creeping thing, and the fowls of the air; for it repented me that I have made them. [Gen. 6:6-7]

As it was in the days before the flood, when people didn't take Noah nor his continued warnings seriously, when God sends the prophets of our generation out with His word of warning today, for the most part, people really don't listen. But just as in the days of Noah, out of His love, God will continue to always send warnings before destruction finally comes. Throughout Scripture, from Genesis to Revelation, we can read about the mercy of God toward mankind and how longsuffering He has been and always will be, until time is up.

When His people sinned against Him, He always sent messengers as a perquisite prior to judgment, and in many cases, they were ignored, laugh at, and sometimes killed. What we are seeing today is the complete rejection of the word of the Lord regarding His absolute judgments, and this is a great tragedy. Sadly, if this continues, many people will be caught unaware of the times we are living in and be eternally lost. The Bible warns that we should not allow the influence of this present world system to cloud our minds, steering us further and further from the truth that is in Christ Jesus [Rom. 12:1-2].

The Bible states that when sin abounds, God's grace abounds much more [Romans 5:20], which literally means that sin will never out do the grace that God provides. I truly believe that when God gave Noah the instructions for the ark, which was the only way of escape from the judgment in that time, He planned it so that there was enough room for a huge amount of people to come on board.

But unfortunately, the people of Noah's day decided not to listen to God's servant, and after God closed the door of the ark, everyone alive on the earth perished because they refused God's only plan of salvation. I'm certain that Noah was laughed at, mocked, rejected, and labeled by the people of his day as a foolish man, out of touch with society, or even a right-wing fanatic.

But according to the Bible, Noah was a just man in the eyes of God and perfect in his generation. After witnessing the moral decline and the hardening hearts of the people toward decency and holiness, in obedience to the voice of God, Noah and his family began to build the ark for the saving of his family. If Noah were alive today, he would have been considered a religious, closed-minded idiot trying to dictate to society how they should live and conduct their lives.

God gave the people in Noah's day ample time to repent of their sins, yet they resisted Him and chose to go with the majority. They chose the pleasures of sin and gambled with their destinies; they died in their sin and were eternally separated from the giver of life forever. They now await in hell the final judgment that will come upon all of those that reject Jesus Christ as Savior and Lord.

Does this sound familiar? The gospel is being proclaimed as never before in our day, and yet people are determined to live a lifestyle of self indulgence, without any fear or regard of God or His Son Jesus Christ. I personally believe that God has done more in our generation than in any other by reaching out to humanity in many different ways. We have the gospel on every form of media known to mankind, and yet many have chosen to play games with their life and leave God completely out of their decisions.

The only prophet of his generation, Noah warned of a coming flood, but no one believed him. It was something that had never happened before, so they mocked him. Their lack of reverence for God grieved God to His heart [Gen. 6:6 KJV].

I'm sure that there were many who thought that God would never punish the creation that He had created. However, the Bible very clearly states that they all, including the animals that were left outside of the ark perished, and that only Noah and his family were saved. What a shame that out of the entire world population of that day, only one family made it out because of their respect for a loving God. Today, God is rising up messengers and prophets like Noah for our generation to sound the trumpet of preparation and the need for dedication to the Lord before His arrival, which is upon us even now!

Jesus made a profound statement regarding the times just prior to His Second Coming when He compared it to the days of Noah:

> But as the days of Noah were, so shall also the coming of the Son of man be. For as in the days that were before the flood they were eating and drinking,

> marrying and giving in marriage, until the day that
> Noah entered into the ark, and knew not until the
> flood came, and took them all away; so shall also the
> coming of the Son of man be. [Matt. 24: 37-39 KJV]

In the days of Noah, there was wickedness everywhere. So God promised to destroy everything He had created on the face of the earth. We have moved into a time like that of Noah, and all over the world, the storm clouds of judgment can already be seen through terrorism, crime, drug abuse, sexual promiscuity, pornography, abortion, and war; the wickedness of man is great, and the love of God is waxing cold. We are truly living in the very last days!

The Bible said that in the last days, people would be more concerned about themselves and the things that pertain to this life than the things of God; when Jesus returns, those who are not prepared won't know, that the actual Rapture event has occurred, it until He has come and gone, and by then, it will be too late for them to repent in order to be included in the great catching away, which is termed the Rapture. In the book of Matthew, Jesus admonishes us to be ready.

> Therefore be ye also ready; for in such an hour as ye
> think not the Son of man cometh. [Matt. 24:44 KJV]

In the Greek, the word translated **"ready"** is a command. The Lord is commanding us to be ready for His return. I believe that by inspiration of the Holy Spirit, Jesus knew what the conditions of the world would be like just prior to His return and asked the question, "When the son of man cometh, will He find faith on the earth?"

If there was ever a time to live by faith, it's now! I remember when I was growing up, I would hear preachers proclaim during altar calls, "Today may be your last day to receive Christ, because tomorrow isn't promised to anyone." They wanted us to know that the coming of Christ was one subject we should take very seriously. The return of Christ to the earth to take His Church into heaven is called the **"blessed hope"** for which all Christians have long awaited. This will be a great event filled with rejoicing for those who love the Lord, but for those who don't know the Lord, it will be a day of great pain, confusion, and misery. As the signs of the time become more evident, something is also happening in the hearts of millions around the world. Fear is taking root.

> And there shall be signs in the sun, and in the moon, and in the stars; and upon the earth distress of nations, with perplexity; the sea and the waves roaring; men's heart failing them for fear, and for looking after those things which are coming on the earth: for the powers of heaven shall be shaken. And then shall they see the Son of man coming in a cloud with power and great glory. [Luke 21:25-27]

The phrase "living in the last days" is not meant to imply that we should be fearful, but faithful. As believers, we should not get caught up in the despair that's in the world; we have a duty to express the very nature of God in the earth by proclaiming the good news of the gospel, which is the hope that we have in Jesus Christ. Jesus said to go into the entire world and preach the good news of the gospel. The only hope for mankind can only be found in Jesus Christ.

Today, there is a great searching in the hearts of people for more than what they have; people are trying everything imaginable to find peace, and true peace can only be found in the one who not only has life, but is life. Jesus said that He is the only way, the truth, and the life; no man could ever reach the Father in heaven without coming through Him.

> Jesus saith unto him, I am the way, the truth, and the life; no man cometh unto the Father, but by me. [John 14:6 KJV]

AMERICA BEFORE 9/11

Before September 11, 2001, life in America was much different than it is today. Prior to September 11, there wasn't much mention of God in the news. As a matter of fact, it was the direct opposite. Across America, people of faith were being verbally persecuted for their faith in God. According to many news reports, which I personally heard, many students in our public school system and colleges across the country were being told that they couldn't pray at school events, even during normal lunch hours, and if they refused, they could be faced with certain consequences!

Some students even received chastisement for the very mention of Jesus Christ in public schools and colleges. Just a few years ago, America was on a very sharp decline morally, spiritually, and economically. Never before in the history of this nation had we seen this type of verbal persecution against the Church, in my opinion. Those who chose to disagree with the opinion of the world system were considered religious fanatics or bigots for simply having another belief.

Many of our church leaders failed to even speak out against certain sins that were prevalent in our society and chose to remain silent. It was disheartening to witness the overall acceptance of the moral decay in our nation and to stand by and watch many of our politicians and national leaders do and say nothing out of fear of being labeled an outsider.

God is love, and He doesn't hate sinners; we are the very reason He gave His only Son. He only hates the sin that's in our heart, and that sin will cause those who reject Jesus as Savior to be eternally separated from His awesome love and God the Father. Some thought that a time of persecution toward the Church in America was on the rise and that we were on the brink of loosing many of the religious freedoms that our forefathers established when America was founded.

Our nation, in my opinion, was on a collision course with America's very foundation. I remember watching TV reports of paintings of Jesus Christ being portrayed in a very harmful and disrespectful manner. It seemed that in many cases, the media had if out for God. America literally forgot that God was watching.

But suddenly, on September 11, 2001, everything changed. That is a day in history that I will never forget. The sadness of that day must never, ever be forgotten, and we must honor the heroes who paid the ultimate sacrifice to protect our freedom. I can take you to the very spot that I was at in my home, and to this very day, I can remember what I was doing at that frightful moment when our TV screens flashed **"Breaking News."** Within moments, three major horrific tragedies shook our entire nation to its core, and the minds of thousands were shattered as planes plunged into the World Trade Center buildings in New York City and the Pentagon in Virginia. A plane headed toward another target, possibly the Capital building in Washington or maybe even the White House, was overtaken by a group of American heroes and went down in a field not far from Washington, DC, resulting in the saving of hundreds of lives.

It was a day when everything in our nation stopped. For many, their view of God was shaken back into reality. An awakening that begun in America in 2001 has continued, and it is spreading around the world. Since that day, many have awakened to the fact that life is more than just the accumulation of things or the pursuit of fancy cars and nice homes. Nothing is wrong with having nice things, but when the things have us, they become idols; God doesn't want that, because He knows that anything that we focus on more than Him will cause us great pain in the end.

America belongs to God; He has a plan for this nation to accomplish before He returns. I personally believe that the plan of God regarding the end-time harvest of souls around the world has begun and that the United States of America will be the key role player God will use.

Since the attacks on September 11, the Bible is now being spoken of all over the world. Many of our major networks are now allowing people of faith who have knowledge of God and the Bible to be interviewed. There seems to be a new openness toward God in America, and many are beginning to realize that the Bible is true and should be studied. Many of our government officials and others in the news media are now discussing the need to allow voluntary prayer back into our public school system.

I believe, along with many others, that if America turns back to God, we will again be feared among the nations, and God will supernaturally protect this nation. As the fear of God starts to come back into the hearts of the people of this country, we will witness the greatest move of God in the history of the United States of America. If the body of Christ takes its position as the only light and spiritual force for good in the earth, God will pour out His Spirit upon our nation, and it will be healed, according to the Word of the God.

> If my people, which are called by my name, shall humble themselves, and pray, and seek my face, and turn from their wicked ways; then will I hear from heaven, and will forgive their sin, and will heal their land. [2 Chron. 7:14]

I believe that this will happen, and as a result of our repenting, a great move of God will come just prior to the coming of the Lord and will demonstrate the most incredible miracles the Church has ever witnessed in all of its history. Mighty signs and wonders are on the horizon, and the people of God will even raise the dead, blind eyes will be opened, and creative miracles will break forth everywhere. It's going to be an exciting time to be alive as the power of God moves from city to city. Satan has played his card of terrorism in an attempt to bring the world to its knees through fear. However, what he meant for evil, God will turn around and use for His glory, if we repent.

Satan will never get the upper hand; he is still a defeated coward. Sometimes it may look as though he is winning, but he's actually losing big-time. According to Scripture, the day of reckoning is coming for him also. This coming move of the Spirit of God will be unprecedented; it will be the book of Acts chapters 4-5 all over again, where miracles, signs and wonders took place, but bigger, and will produce more souls won into the kingdom of God.

I truly believe that we have been given a serious wakeup call from the tragedy that took place on 9/11, and now that the Body of Christ is awakened, God is going to move upon us like never before. There have been reports from men of God throughout the country that during this awakening, entire cities will come to the Lord, as the glory of God descends upon His saints.

I believe that God is going to use young people mightily in this coming move of His Spirit.

AMERICA'S HEDGE OF PROTECTION

*O*ne of my most favorite stories in the Bible regarding divine protection is found in the book of Job. Job feared the Lord and really placed God first in his life. He was a man of integrity and raised his family on the principles of God, and as a result of his love and respect for God, the Lord protected Job and all of his possessions with a hedge of protection. This hedge of protection couldn't be seen with the natural eye, but the effects of it could be seen.

Job was extremely wealthy and had plenty of goods. Not only was Job blessed, but his children were blessed. Everything connected to Job was blessed and favored by God in a very tremendous way. The Bible tells us that Job was perfect and upright before God and eschewed evil [Job 1:1 KJV].

This was a man who hated evil with a pure hatred and was honored by the God of heaven. As God took care of Job, He also protected Israel. Whenever Israel was faithful to God, He protected them and didn't allow any of the enemies that surrounded them to attack or defeat them. Their obedience to God kept them divinely protected from harm. And just like Israel of old, the nations of the world that fear the Lord and the United States of America have this same type of hedge of protection. America has had its share of problems and hasn't lived up to the so-called Christian nation label, but America has been the leading nation who has taken the gospel of Jesus Christ to the nations of the world.

But the great sins of our nation and the tide of wickedness that is currently proceeding from it could cause the hedge of God's supernatural protection to be lifted, if we aren't careful to get back in God's good favor. Decades of disrespect toward God and His Word are the culprit that will unleash the judgment of the Lord upon not just America but every nation that forgets God.

> The wicked shall be turned back [headlong, into premature death] into sheol [place of departed spirits of the wicked]; even all the nations that forget or are forgetful of God. [Psalm 9:17]

Prior to September 11, the Church in America had been asleep for years, resting in the arms of comfort and prosperity. But God is not mocked; whatsoever a person sows, that is exactly what he or she will reap. I personally knew within my own heart that America was in trouble, by the reports that were coming from evangelical leaders in the Body of Christ regarding the level of sensitivity toward some of the basic fundamentals of the Christian experience, like winning the lost.

The evangelical movement of the Church had come to a literal halt as many of God's people kept the message of Jesus Christ within the four walls of their own congregations. The impact the Church once had on communities across America had weakened and was nearly nonexistent in some areas.

In many ways, the Church was really starting to look more and more like the un-churched. Compromise within the pulpit had also reached an all-time high. There was even talk in some denominations regarding the acceptance of all forms of lifestyles, even those that the Bible warns against. Some were even considered as normal and accepted. The truth of the Word that was once respected was now being turned into lies, just as the apostle Paul warns in the book of Romans.

Paul starts out by addressing the condition of a church that was backslidden and lukewarm.

> Because when they knew and recognized him as God, they did not honor and glorify him as God or give him thanks. But instead they became futile and godless in their thinking (with vain imaginings, foolish reasoning, and stupid speculations) and their senseless minds were darkened. Claiming to be wise, they became fools, professing to be smart, they made simpletons of themselves. And by them the glory and majesty and excellence of the immortal God is exchanged for the represented by images, resembling mortal man and birds and beasts and reptiles. Therefore God gave them up in the lust of their own hearts to sexual impurity, to the dishonoring of their bodies among themselves, abandoning them to the degrading power of sin. Because they exchanged the truth of God for a lie and worshipped and served the creature rather than the Creator, who is blessed forever! Amen. For this reason God gave them over and abandoned them to vile affections and degrading passions. For

their women exchanged their natural function for an unnatural and abnormal one, and the men also turned from natural relations with women and were set ablaze, burning out, consumed with lust for one another, men committing shameful acts with men and suffering in their own bodies and personalities the inevitable consequences and penalty of their wrong-doing and going astray, which was their fitting retribution. [Rom. 1:21-27 AMP]

In the book of Isaiah, we see an example of how the Lord relates to His Church. Notice how the Lord compares His people to a garden.

Now will I sing to my well beloved a song of my beloved touching his vineyard. My well beloved hath a vineyard in a very fruitful hill: And he fenced it, and gathered out the stones thereof, and planted it with the choicest vine, and built a tower in the midst of it, and also make a winepress therein: and he looked that it should bring forth grapes, and it brought forth wild grapes. [Isa. 5:1-6]

The Lord made certain that several things were in place to ensure that His garden, the Church, flourished and had good results in the latter end. He began the work in a fruitful hill; He planted His garden in a good environment, where the soil was rich. He then fenced it about; He placed protection around His assets and separated it unto himself.

"Gather out the stones thereof" means that He removed all the obstacles and anything that would hinder His garden's growth. He planted it with the choicest vine, which was the best of the best, His only Son. He built a tower in the midst thereof—a place of refuge. He placed a winepress inside of it, which was used to press the grapes into fine wine.

Much work went into the planting of this garden. The Lord was expecting results from this vineyard because of the efforts made in planting it, just as He does of His Church. However, when it was time for the vineyard to produce, it brought forth wild grapes. Why did the vineyard that the Lord planted yield wild grapes?

Let's consider the facts: the soil was good, the environment in which the work was started was good, the vine was perfect, and it was fenced in and protected from any outside distractions. Yet at the time of harvest, the results that God was looking for weren't there.

I won't pretend to have all the answers as to why we as God's dear children aren't bearing the kind of fruit that God is looking for; I can only tell you about why I, as a born again Christian, fail the Lord and for years didn't bear any fruit at all. I was under the impression that since I was saved and had confessed my sins, there wasn't anything else that was needed for me to do. I had no idea that God didn't just save me for me. He brought me out of the world system and it's lust, in order to bring others into the things of God.

I didn't have a clue that without a personal ongoing relationship with the Lord, it would be difficult to live a consistent Christian life dedicated to God in this wicked world system. Jesus said that if we don't abide in Him, we won't be able to do anything for Him, and neither will He be able to do anything through us (John 15:4); I learned that the hard way. Proverbs 6:16-19 mentions seven things that the Lord hates, and many of these hateful things are present in the lives of many of God's children, causing them to not be fruitful in their relationship with God.

> These six things doth the Lord hate; yea, seven are an abomination unto him: A proud look, a lying tongue, and hands that shed innocent blood, an heart that devises wicked imaginations, feet that be swift in running to mischief, a false witness that speaks lies, and he that soweth discord among the brethren. [Prov. 6:16-19 KJV]

When sin is in the heart, it stops growth and productivity in the things of God. Sin in the life of a believer will cause the seed of God's Word to not grow and produce Godly results. When God raised up the Church in America, it was for a divine purpose. America's protection and future doesn't rest on the shoulders of our government nor our awesome military, but in Christ Jesus alone.

The Bible declares that we are the salt (the preservative) of the earth; we know that salt not only preserves, but irritates, and God has called us to do both. We are also the light of the world. In the diaries of the founder of our great nation, Christopher Columbus wrote that he was compelled to sail west by the "inspiration of the Holy Spirit."

He continued, "It was the Lord who put into my mind, I could feel His hand upon me, the fact that it would be possible to sail from here to the Indies." America was God's idea from the beginning, and its foundation was built upon the Word of God. Our strength and security can only be found in God. In Psalm 11:3, the Bible makes it very clear that "if the foundations be destroyed, what can the righteous do?"

Kicking God out of society isn't very smart, yet every day, millions of Americans, and some of our political leaders, are doing just that. The same scenario that we read about in Isaiah chapter five is the same one we see being played out in America today. God has abundantly blessed America with wealth and untold riches due to our founding; our nation was founded upon biblical principles.

America is blessed because of its heritage in God Almighty. Because of this firm foundation, America has become the greatest nation on the face of the earth and, as it stands, the only super power left that can use its influence to make the world a much better place than it is right now. America has stood as a beacon of light for millions.

Tens of thousands of people from all over the world risk their very lives just to place their foot on American soil; they desire to partake of the freedoms we have enjoyed for over two hundred years. I personally believe that God divinely placed a supernatural hedge around America to protect it. America has been a blessing to many nations around the world, especially to the nation of Israel; God Himself said that He would bless those who bless Israel and curse those who curse Israel, and America has been a solid friend of Israel for decades.

All that we have done right can't remove the fact that since the mid-1970s, we've seen a great turning to evil by the general population in America, especially the youth, with abortions, pornography, drug abuse, neglect of children, rape, incest, and lately, a great turning away from the things of God by those who say that Jesus is Lord of their lives.

This really shouldn't come as a surprise to us if we've read the warnings of the apostle Paul when he declared that "in the last days," just prior to the coming of the Lord, many would depart from the faith, giving heed to seducing spirits and doctrines of demons [1 Timothy 4:1]. We are presently in that time right now, and this scripture is coming to pass right before our eyes. I believe that the sins of omission and commission, along with inconsistencies within the Church, have brought about the removing or lifting of the hedge of God's supernatural protection from America, and this may have been the real reason behind 9/11. God is not the author of death — Satan is — but when God's people turn from Him, sin and death are bound to take over.

In order to get the hedge restored, we must repent and allow the fear of God to come back into our lives as believers. Everything is resting upon the Church — the body that God is depending on in order to change things for our nation and the world. In 2 Chronicles 7:13-14 KJV, the Lord declares,

> When I shut up heaven and there is no rain, or command the locust to devour the land, or send pestilence among my people, if my people who are called by my name will humble themselves, and pray, and seek my face, and turn from their wicked ways, then will I hear from heaven, and will forgive their sin and heal their land.

We must always remember that God is a loving God, slow to anger and bountiful in mercy and love. God is always willing and ready to forgive. The Father's will is that none perish or see lack and defeat. God is a good God, and He is always looking for ways to bless His creation. But unless He has our hearts, life will be hard and difficult. We were created for Him and for His pleasure, and until we really come to that reality, Satan will always have the upper hand.

WATCHING

"Watch therefore (which means give strict attention, be cautious and active), for you don't know in what kind of a day (whether a near or remote one) your Lord is coming" [Matt. 24:42 AMP]. In this hour, God is commanding His people to watch continuously because we don't know the hour of His eminent return. Some have made the mistake in thinking that if you believe in the sudden coming of the Lord, there is no real reason to prepare for a future in this present time by investing, going to college, getting married, making long-term commitments to your family by purchasing life insurance, etc.

This is a mistake in judgment because Jesus said that we ought to occupy, which means to do business and be useful and productive until He comes. We ought to live our lives every day as though Jesus could return at any moment, but also look forward to being here another one hundred years. The Bible says that nobody on earth can ever know the day or the hour in which our Lord will return, and anyone who attempts to lock down a date or time will always come up short because the day and the hour is only known by the Father, not even the angels; it's a secret. However, it's the responsibility of every Christian to live his or her life in accordance with God's Word, so that when Jesus dose come, he or she will be ready.

In the book of Titus, we are admonished to look for Christ's return. "Looking for that blessed hope, and the glorious appearing of the great God and our Savior Jesus Christ" [Titus 2:13 KJV]. In the book of Hebrews, Paul declares that Jesus will appear unto them who are looking for Him. "So Christ was once offered to bear the sins of many; and unto them that look for him shall he appear the second time without sin unto salvation" [Heb. 9:28 KJV].

As we witness the signs of the times, every believer in the Lord Jesus Christ should be looking and waiting for the return of the Lord. This is not escapism, as some call it; it's simply Bible-based theology. Jesus said that the generation alive to see the rebirth of the nation of Israel, which occurred in June of 1948, would not pass away, but that generation would be alive to see the fulfillment of all things pertaining to the last days [Matt. 24:32-34 KJV].

In 2 Timothy 3:1-5, we are warned that in the last days, there would be people who have a form of godliness but deny or reject the power thereof. As we look forward to the greatest move of the Holy Spirit the Church has ever known, we also see this tragic prophecy coming to pass right before our eyes.

Paul said that this group of people who profess to be believers would have just a form of godliness—everything on the outside looks good, but the inside is corrupt. They would know how to say all the right religious terms, look spiritual outwardly, but lack the inward witness of the Holy Spirit that produces Godly results.

They are one thing in public, but behind closed doors, they are another person entirely. Today, we unfortunately have skilled, professional church-goers. They know how to preach, sing, and dance, but outside of the four walls of the church, they are living out a totally different lifestyle that is contrary to the Word of God.

Timothy said that these are the kind of people who go place to place committing acts in their flesh that unbelievers participate in. He also said that they are very quick to get to the next seminar to learn about the things of God, but they will never be able to come to the knowledge of the truth. This is a tragedy in the Body of Christ. It's time that we understand that learning about God and knowing Him are two entirely different things.

We have moved into a time when some can't endure sound doctrine but, after their own lust, heap to themselves teachers having itching ears. Jesus made a very profound statement in Matthew chapter seven that sent chills through my body when I read it for the first time many years ago. He said, "Not everyone that said unto me, Lord, Lord shall enter into the kingdom of heaven; but only he that doeth the will of my Father which is in heaven" [Matt. 7:21 KJV].

According to this verse, just the mere confession that Jesus is Lord without the actions to back it up isn't sufficient enough for a person to be allowed entrance into heaven. Therefore, based on this scripture, we know that believing in God isn't enough. The Bible tells us that the even the demons of hell and Satan both believe that there is a God and tremble as a result of that knowledge.

The Greek word for "believe" means more than just a mere mental assent; it means a commitment of one's life. Believing that God is isn't enough. The Bible states that faith without works is dead [James 2:20]. If we really believe that Jesus is Lord, there should be some corresponding action in our life to verify that belief.

There are some who think that they can live any way they choose and just come to church and say, "Lord, I'm sorry," and be forgiven without any remorse or change of heart. Our God is a merciful God and will forgive every single time we ask Him, if we are sincere. God isn't looking for a simple "I'm sorry, Lord" week after week without a mind or will to change. He demands total obedience and commitment to His Son. This is the reason we have pastors, teachers, evangelists, prophets, and apostles—they are for our learning and spiritual development.

The Lord understands that we are weak in our flesh; He is very patience with us, as any father would be toward his children. However, there comes a time when we, as children of God, must grow up into mature Christians. I've personally had struggles in many areas of my life that caused great pain and distress, but it wasn't until I finally gave up and said, "Lord, I can't do this anymore in my own ability," when Jesus stepped into my situation and changed things for good.

When we place our total trust in what Jesus did on the cross two thousand years ago, we will begin to walk in the liberty and freedom only found in Him. God demands holiness, for He is Holy.

The Bible says, "Be ye Holy, for I am Holy" [1 Pet. 1:16 KJV]. Being holy isn't a suggestion from the Lord; it's a command from the commander and chief of heaven. We are also told in Scripture that without holiness, no man shall see the Lord. We are living in a time of the greatest deception the Church has ever witnessed.

The response we are seeing in the area of personal evangelism in the Body of Christ is shocking; the numbers are staggering. In some locations, churches are filling up with people from other churches; I call it church hopping—when you get offended at something that happen or was said at your church, you can simply switch memberships, and as a result, we are failing to reach the harvest because we've become so very carnal. When the world looks at the Church today, they don't see much light.

In many of our churches in America, only when a guest singer or a famous speaker comes are the congregations filled to standing room only, but when it comes to meeting for prayer, all you find is a handful of the faithful, who are holding things together by their faithfulness to pray while the others seem to be preoccupied with things that really have no spiritual significance toward God.

Some would rather be entertained than fed spiritual food from the Word of God. Many churches that have evangelical outings barely get enough people to participate in the program to win souls to Christ. Many of the good intentions that some have regarding evangelism die in the infant stages because there isn't enough support. This is a tragedy, and other religions are making a mark in our day, especially with the young people, because the leadership in some of our churches can't discern the times in which we are living.

On the other hand, we hear many screaming in the face of God for blessings, riches, and things that pertain to this the natural realm. How pitiful we must look in the eyes of the martyrs, who were eaten by lions, stoned, jailed, and even nailed to crosses for their faith in Christ. Those who lived before us knew what it was to give up something for Christ; they knew firsthand what it meant to die to the things of this natural world and completely sell out to Christ.

If we are going to see that mighty move of the Spirit that was promised for the last days, we'd better repent and become consecrated and dedicated to the things of God.

ANOTHER WAVE OF SHAKINGS

I, along with many other church leaders, believe that the world is on the brink of another wave of shaking from the presence of the Lord, both in the natural realm and the spiritual realm. When some hear the term "shaking," they immediately think something bad is going to happen, but in most cases, when God begins to shake things, what He's really doing is bringing in changes that will better serve His eternal purposes. God sees things in light of eternality.

The natural shakings that will occur and are occurring right now will be things that can be seen, like national leadership. When God is about to do something on earth, He chooses men or women to occupy places of authority so that in the end, His plans can be established. We see this in the life of Saul, who habitually disobeyed the God of Israel, so God chose David to reign in his stead. God actually brought things in motion in the natural realm to bring about Saul's downfall.

> And he changeth the times and the seasons; he removeth kings, and setteth up kings; he giveth wisdom unto the wise, and knowledge to them that know understanding. [Dan. 2:21 KJV]

God is going to shake everything that can be shaken, and He will continue to do so until our trust is solely in Him alone; this includes anything that we, individually or as a nation, are holding onto more than Him. Some may ask, what makes America so special? Why would God shake America? The answer to that question is very simple. America was founded on biblical principles, and the founding fathers of our nation all spoke openly about the God of Abraham, Isaac, and Jacob. When our nation was founded, God was at the centerpiece, and there wasn't any talk about the separation of church and state. Our founding fathers all had a relationship with the God of the Bible.

When touring Washington, DC, with a prayer group back in 2007, I noticed that all of the monuments we visited had writings attributed to Almighty God on them or beside them. Some in our group, including myself, even sensed a wonderful presence of the Lord as we read the verbiage written by our past leaders about their experience with God. So when I talk about coming shakings, it's due to the fact that since our nation was founded by God, He has the right and the ability to bring correction when we get out of line with His plans.

Some have said that the magnitude economic shakings of 1929 would never happen again, but according to Scripture, what occurred in the United States in 1929 will one day be global, and according to the book of Revelation, written by the apostle John, a day that famine will shake the entire planet is on the horizon.

> And I heard the voice in the midst of the four beasts
> say, a measure of wheat for a penny and three mea-
> sures of barley for a penny; see thou hurt not the oil
> and the wine. [Rev. 6:6]

A measure was about one quart, a slave's daily ration, and the amount usually purchased for about two cents. One could usually buy eight measures of wheat or twenty-four measures of barley for a penny, but during this future famine, only one measure of wheat or three measures of barley can be purchased for a penny. This will make food eight times higher than in normal times.

The economies of the world are already being shaken by terrorism; natural disasters, such as hurricanes, earthquakes, and tsunamis; and other cataclysmic events around the globe. Whatever we trust in more than God will be shaken. For years without end, hundreds of thousands have had their complete confidence and trust in the economy and the stock market, not in the living God.

Now, please don't misunderstand me right here, because there is absolutely nothing wrong with investing and saving money. However, we must not allow our investment portfolios and our saving accounts to replace our dependency in the living God. We must always remember that God is a jealous God, and He not only wants first place in our lives, but He also desires for us to be wholly unto Him. "Thou shall have no other gods before me" [Gen. 20:3]; that includes the god of money.

THE COMING WEALTH TRANSFER

The greatest move of God to ever hit the earth is presently upon us, and I believe we haven't even seen anything compared to what God is going to do in the very near future as His glory begins to invade our very lives. The Church has seen many moves of the Spirit of God since the day of Pentecost, but the move that is coming will be spectacular in the area of our finances. I believe that the real Church is ripe for this move of divine blessing.

This blessing won't be based upon anyone's own righteousness or self effort, but just because it's time. We have seen mighty moves of the Spirit in the realm of healings, miracles, and evangelism. But what we haven't seen is a breakthrough in the financial realm. God's will is that His people are the head and not the tail, above only and never beneath. One of the keys that will unlock the door to supernatural abundance in our lives is obedience.

Some have the idea that Jesus can't come back until every single believer is financially blessed and living a prosperous life. It would be wonderful if the entire Body of Christ could grasp the true message of biblical prosperity, which flows from within, and begin to live in the blessings of God. But unfortunately, that won't be the case. If we had to wait for everyone in the Church to believe in and accept the message of prosperity before the Lord comes, the coming of the Lord would be delayed indefinitely. There are some in the Church who really don't like to hear about money, yet they are the very ones who need it the most. I personally believe that money has a purpose in this last hour. In addition, the time has come for the resources that God has placed in the earth to be used in the service of His Kingdom.

The Bible speaks of a time to come when those that have trusted in their riches and have made wealth their god will come into great misery. I believe that this time is upon us now.

> Go to now, ye rich men, weep and howl for your miseries that shall come upon you. Your riches are corrupted, and your garments are moth-eaten. Your gold and silver is cankered; and the rust of them shall be a witness against you and shall eat your flesh, as it were fire. Ye have heaped treasure together for the last days. [James 5:1-3]

Here the Bible declares that treasure or money has been heaped up, stored up, or kept back for the last days, and we are presently living in the last days. For years I've understood [James 5:1-3] in the Scripture to speak about the Church being blessed so that it can be a blessing to others, yet many in the Church can't bless anyone, because they themselves aren't financially blessed.

There are many reasons why some in the Body of Christ haven't seen the blessing of God in the area of finances. Obedience in the area of giving is a big reason why many are living below their privileges as kings and priests.

Tithing, which is 10 percent of our gross income, is a biblical principle, yet many don't tithe. As a result, the devourer, who is the devil, has been given free access into their lives to destroy their finances. In the book of Malachi, God makes the following statements:

[Even from the days of your fathers ye are gone away from mine ordinances, and have not kept them. Return unto me, and I will return unto you, saith the Lord of host. But ye said, Wherein shall we return? Will a man rob God? Yet ye have robbed me, but ye say, Wherein have we robbed thee? In tithes and offerings. Ye are cursed with a curse; for ye have robbed me, even this whole nation Mal. 3:7-9].

In this portion of Scripture, the Lord said that an entire nation was cursed because they didn't honor Him and robbed Him twice by not paying their tithe or their offerings. Tithing is a biblical principle that works. My family has been tremendously blessed because of our commitment to God to tithe 10 percent of our gross income. God has always been faithful, and He has never let us down in any area of our lives since becoming a family that tithes.

Tithing isn't something that we do; it's who we are. Some think that tithing was only for the Old Testament, and I assure you that we could argue over this point until the Lord returns. But if you really want to know my true feelings about this, I can sum it up in a few words: it's a heart thing. Tithing is supported in Scripture, both the Old and New Testaments. Once, I asked the Lord about why we are taught to give and give continually; He reminded me that giving is the nature of God, and if God is truly in us, we will be givers.

In the book of Malachi, it declares that those who don't honor the Lord in tithes and offerings will be cursed with a curse. When we fail to tithe, we give the devil and his demons an open door into our finances. We must be careful not to take out portions of the Word of God that we don't agree with and keep the ones that we do agree with; this is what I call selective obedience. God also promised that if we obeyed His Word regarding tithing, He would rebuke or hold back the devil from operating in our lives.

Satan will not be able to destroy what belongs to us if we give God what belongs to Him. In these last days, the purpose of money is and always has been to spread the good news of the gospel of Jesus Christ to the nations of the world. When the Church turns its focus back to winning the lost, God will open up the floodgates of heaven and bless His saints with financial blessings beyond anything we could dream of or imagine.

I don't know about you, but I would much rather be on the receiving end of God's blessings rather than the curse. God won't pour out money from heaven, but He will empower us with ideas and skills to get wealth in order to bring about His plan for mankind and the fulfillment of His word.

> But thou shalt remember the Lord thy God: for it
> is he that giveth thee power to get wealth that he
> may establish his covenant which he sware unto thy
> fathers, as it is this day. [Deut. 8:18 KJV]

It going to take multiple millions of dollars to complete the task the Lord Jesus gave to the Church when He commanded, "Go ye into all the world, and preach the gospel to every creature." [Mark 15:15]

When we put the gospel of Jesus Christ first, then and only then will the Lord begin to add to our lives. Jesus made it very clear where our priorities should be when He said,

> But seek ye first the kingdom of God and his righteousness: and all these thins shall be added unto you. [Matt. 6:33 KJV]

When we make God's kingdom our priority instead of things and possessions, life takes on a whole new meaning. When the Body of Christ begins to realize the power of giving to the work of God to reach the masses, working from nine to five will no longer be a drag; it will become exciting, and employers everywhere will begin to wonder what's going on with those employees who say that they love Jesus Christ.

When we take on the attitude that we are actually partnering with God in getting His Word out to the lost, God will show us how to make our money serve us. We must never forget that the true purpose of wealth and financial prosperity is to fulfill the promise God made to Abraham many thousands of years ago, when He said,

Get this out of thy country, and from thy kindred, and from thy fathers house, unto a land that I will show thee, and I will make thee a great nation, and will bless thee, and make thy name great; and thou shall be a blessing:

> And I will bless them that bless thee, and curse them that curse thee: and in thee shall all of the families of the earth be blessed [Gen. 12:1-3].

After God changed Abram's name to Abraham, He made a covenant between Himself and Abraham, promising that He would multiply him exceedingly. God vowed to take care of Abraham and his descendants in every area of life.

In the book of Galatians, the Bible declares that if we are Christ's, then we are Abraham's seed and heirs according to the promises that God made to Abraham [Gal. 3:29]. We must understand that by faith, we are the seed of Abraham, and whatever God promised to Abraham can literally be applied to us also if we obey God and keep His word as Abraham did.

This is why we must obey God where money is concerned and why paying our tithe unto the Lord is a must. Let's not allow ten cents of a dollar keep us back from the financial blessings of heaven. If you haven't been tithing faithfully, repent and become a tither today, and watch your heavenly Father make you a blessing.

Now is the time to give to the Lord's work. Very soon, the Lord is going to rapture His Church from the earth, and after the Rapture, everything regarding how money is used will become drastically different. During the great Tribulation period, money as we know it and its use will be discontinued. According to the book of Revelation, when the antichrist makes his push for world dominance, he will institute a new method of commerce, and it will be his mark.

> And he causeth all, both small and great, rich and poor,
> free and bond, to receive a mark in their right hand or
> in their foreheads: And that no man might buy or sell,
> save he that had the mark, or the name of the beast, or
> the number of his name. [Rev. 13:16-17 KJV]

As you have just read, money will only be significant during the Church age. When the Church is gone, the mark of the beast system will be instituted for daily commerce. We are nearing the end of the Age of Grace, and our giving to God will be directly responsible for reaching millions around the world. This is the true reason why God desires us to be blessed. We must remember, financial abundance is not about our comfort and wellbeing in this life alone, and it never has been; it's about the covenant that God made with Abraham, that all the families of the earth would be blessed [Gen. 12:3].

The greatest gift that we can give to any person is the gospel of Jesus Christ, and when we take what God has blessed us with and sow it into the harvest, God is honored because we are literally using our money to win souls. This is also fulfilling the great commission that Jesus gave to the Church just before He ascended on high.

> Go ye into all the world, and preach the gospel to every creature. He that believeth and is baptized shall be saved; but he that believeth not shall be damned. [Mark 16:15-16]

THE RAPTURE

*T*he next major prophetic event that will take the world, and many in the Church, by surprise and propel the world into a time of great horror and sadness will be the glorious Rapture of the Church. The Rapture of the Church will be an event the world has never witnessed before. It will stop the normal flow of operations around the world suddenly and without warning, as people from every nation on earth will vanish.

> Behold I show you a mystery; we shall not all sleep,
> but we shall all be changed, in a moment, in the
> twinkling of an eye, at the last trump; for the trumpet
> shall sound, and the dead shall be raised incorrupt-
> ible, and we shall be changed. [1 Cor. 15:51-52]

The actual word "rapture" is taken from a fourth century Latin translation of the word "harpazo," which means being caught up or violently taken away. Every believer who has died and gone to heaven before us will rise from his or her grave. Their bodies will be reunited with their spirit in heaven, and they will appear with Christ in the clouds. Those of us that are presently in Christ Jesus here on the earth will then be changed in the twinkling of an eye;

we will then be caught up in the air to meet the Lord above the clouds. What a day that's going to be.

> But I would not have you to be ignorant, brethren, concerning them, which are asleep, that ye sorrow not even as others, which have no hope. For if we believe that Jesus died and rose again, even so them also which sleep in Jesus will God bring with him. For this we say unto you by the Word of the Lord, that we, which are alive and remain unto the coming of the Lord, shall not prevent them, which are asleep. For the Lord Himself shall descend from heaven with a shout, with the voice of the archangel, and with the trump of God: and the dead in Christ shall rise first: Then we which are alive and remain shall be caught up together with them in the clouds, to meet the Lord in the air: and so shall we ever be with the Lord. [1 Thess. 4:16-18 KJV]

There are some who teach against a literal Rapture, but the Word of God declares that it's going to happen. Ready or not, Jesus is coming to take His Church out of the earth before the great judgments of the Tribulation begin. Therefore, it behooves us who name Jesus Christ as Savior and Lord to be watching and ready, expecting the Lord to return at any moment.

MISCONCEPTIONS REGARDING THE RAPTURE

*T*here are several misconceptions regarding the timing of the Rapture. I personally believe in a pre-Tribulation Rapture and will show you why according to the Scriptures. Jesus will not leave His people here on the earth while the waft of God is being poured out. The first misconception that some have is that Jesus can't rapture the Church until His bride is ready, which some have concluded is the Body of Christ. I agree that the Church is the bride of Christ, but there is also another meaning given in Scripture for the bride.

> And there came unto me one of the seven angels which had the seven vials full of the seven last plagues, and talked with me, saying, come hither, I will show thee the bride, the Lamb's wife. And he carried me away in the spirit to a great and high mountain, and showed me that great city, the holy Jerusalem, descending out of heaven from God, having the glory of God; and her light was like unto a stone most precious, even like a jasper stone, clear as crystal. [Rev. 21:9-11]

In certain scriptures in the Bible, Jesus refers to the saints as His bride. However, we must be careful not to put more into the Scripture than what is written. When I think of a bride, I think of something beautiful, white, clean, and pure, and that's how Jesus wants His people to live, in pure holiness; as a matter of fact, God demands purity and holiness in our relationship with Him. From the beginning, He knew that we were incapable of living up to His high moral standards, which is why He sent Jesus to be the one that would stand in our stead and pay the price for our sins.

And now, because of the finished work of Christ, God doesn't see our faults and failures as He once did; He looks at us through the blood of His only begotten Son and declares us righteous. When we confess our sins to Him, the Lord gives us the power that enables us to walk in the finished work of the cross.

> Wherefore, as by one man sin entered into the world, and death by sin; and so death passed upon all men, for that all have sinned: For until the law sin was in the world, but sin is not imputed when there is no law. Nevertheless death reigned from Adam to Moses, even over them that had not sinned after the similitude of Adam's transgression, who is the figure of him that was to come. But not as the offence, so also is the free gift, for if through the offence of one many be dead, much more the grace of God, and the gift by grace, which is by one man, Jesus Christ, hath abounded unto many. And not as it was by one that sinned, so is the gift; for the judgment was by one to condemnation, but the free gift

is of many offences unto justification. For if by one man's offence death reined by one; much more they which receive abundance of grace and of the gift of righteousness shall reign in life by one, Jesus Christ.

Therefore as by the offence of one judgment came upon all men to condemnation; even so by the righteousness of one the free gift came upon all men unto justification of life. For as by one man's disobedience many were made sinners, so by the obedience of one shall many be made righteous? Moreover the law entered, that the offence might abound. But where sin abounded, grace did much more abound. That as sin hath reigned unto death, even so might grace reign through righteousness unto eternal life by Jesus Christ our Lord. [Rom. 5:12-21]

Only through the blood of Jesus are we made the righteousness of God and no longer stand guilty before Him. Because of what Jesus did nearly two thousand years ago, Heaven is speaking on behalf of those that have received Jesus as Lord. And right now, in Christ Jesus, we literally stand before God as though we have never sinned. This is the beauty of the gospel.

Even the righteousness of God, which is by faith of Jesus Christ unto all and upon all them that believe, for there is no difference. For all have sinned and come short of the glory of God. Being justified freely by His grace through the redemption that is in Christ Jesus. [Rom. 3:22-24]

The Church is looked upon as the Lord's bride and referred to as His bride because of the blood of Jesus that has made us free and washed our sins away. God isn't going to take the Church through some type of purging process to get us clean in the Tribulation. He's already done that through the cross of Calvary. As Jesus said on the cross before He yielded up His spirit, "It is finished." [John 19:30]

The second misconception that some believe is that Jesus can't rapture the Church until everyone living has an opportunity to hear the gospel at least once. We must understand that the original call to preach the gospel to the world was given to the descendents of Abraham, which are the Jewish people before and after the resurrection [Matt. 28:19-20]. However, when the Jewish people missed their day of visitation, God rose up the gentile Church, not to replace Israel but to preach the Kingdom of God to the ends of the earth.

> If thou hardest known, even thou, at least in this thy day, the things which belong unto thy peace! But they are hid from thine eyes. For the days shall come upon thee, that thine enemies shall cast a trench about thee, and compass thee round, and keep thee in on every side. And shall lay thee even with the ground, and thy children within thee, and they shall not leave in thee one stone upon another; because thou knewest not the time of thy visitation. [Luke 19:42-44]

Immediately after the Rapture of the Church, the Lord will pour out His Spirit on 144,000 of the seed of Abraham, the Jewish people, and use them to complete the work the gentile Church had started before the Rapture. Twelve thousand Jews from each of the twelve tribes of Israel will proclaim the gospel of the kingdom of God for three and a half years into the Tribulation Period, and multitudes will be saved during this time of revival. Jewish believers began sending the Word of God to the nations of the world, and this task will be completed by Jewish believers following the Rapture of the Church. The Rapture can actually take place at any moment.

> And after these things I saw four angels standing on the four corners of the earth, holding the four winds of the earth, that the wind should not blow on the earth, nor on the sea, nor on any tree. And I saw another angel ascending from the east, having the seal of the living God: and he cried with a loud voice to the four angels, to whom it was given to hurt the earth and the sea. Saying hurt not the earth, neither the sea, nor the trees, tell we have sealed the servants of our God in their foreheads. And I heard the number of them, which were sealed: and there were sealed an hundred and forty and four thousand of all the tribes of the children of Israel. [Rev. 7:1-4]

Another misconception regarding the timing of the Rapture is that Jesus can't Rapture the Church until the restitution of all things has been has been fulfilled. The word "restitution" is translated from the Greek word "apokatastasis," which means a complete restoration or reestablishment.

> Having made known unto us the mystery of his will, according to his good pleasure which he hath purposed in himself: That in the dispensation of the fullness of times he might gather together in one all things in Christ both which are in heaven, and which are on earth even in him. [Eph. 1:10 KJV]

Christ Jesus is presently about His Father's business, which is the restoration and redemption of mankind to God. Following the Rapture and the completion of the great Tribulation Period, the millennial reign of Jesus Christ will begin, when the Lord will present this entire planet along with the saints to His Father.

> Then cometh the end, when he shall have delivered up the kingdom to God, even the Father; when he shall have put down all rule and all authority and power. For he must reign, till he hath put all enemies under his feet. The last enemy that shall be destroyed is death. For he hath put all things under his feet. But when he saith all things are put under him, it is manifest that he is excepted, which did put all things under him. And when all things shall be subdued unto him, then shall the Son also himself be subject unto him that put all things under him, that God may be all in all. [1 Cor. 15:24-28 KJV]

Christ's mission was not only to restore man back to His original place in God, but also to restore all things back to God the Father, as they were before the fall of Lucifer. In the beginning, when God created the heavens and the earth, He didn't create the earth without form; neither was the earth void. In Genesis 1:1, the word for "earth" in the original Greek language is "erets," which means ground or land. But as we can see, something cataclysmic took place between the first and second verses in the first chapter of Genesis.

In Genesis 1:2, the Bible says that the earth was without form and void. The word "was" in the original is defined as became. So the earth that God created was perfect until Lucifer fell, and then the earth became without form and void. Some Bible scholars believe that Isaiah 24:1 has a dull meaning and could refer to the time when Lucifer was thrown out of heaven.

After Lucifer rebelled against God, the perfect order of things was interrupted by sin, which was found in the heart of Lucifer, a high-ranking angel who was mighty before God and had influence in the heavens. Jesus Christ, the Son of the living God, is going to restore the heavens and the earth, and Satan will be bound forever in outer darkness forever and forever. This will fulfill the restitution of all things.

> And the devil that deceived them was cast into the lake of fire and brimstone, where the beast and the false prophet are, and shall be tormented day and night forever and ever. [Rev. 20:10]

After this complete restoration of all things, God will dwell with man forever and ever. This is the reason why Jesus can't physically come back to the earth—all things have not yet been restored to Him. You see, my friends, Christ can't come back to the earth with the Church until the restitution of all things are fulfilled, but He can and will come back in the clouds in the Rapture to take His people from the earth. This is the mystery that has been hidden from many but is now being made known by the Holy Ghost and the Word. The second coming of Christ has two parts to it: first, Jesus comes for His Church, then seven years later, He comes back with His Church [Thess. 4:16-18].

THE MYSTERY OF THE TEN VIRGINS

Then the Kingdom of heaven shall be likened to ten virgins who took their lamps and went to meet the bridegroom, five of them were foolish (thoughtless, without forethought) and five were wise (sensible, intelligent, and prudent), for when the foolish took their lamps, they did not take any (extra) oil with them; but the wise took flasks of oil along with them (also) with their lamps. While the bridegroom lingered and was slow in coming, they all began nodding their heads, and they fell asleep. But at midnight there was a shout, "Behold, the bridegroom! Go out to meet him!" Then all those virgins got up and put their own lamps in order. And the foolish said to the wise, "Give us some of your oil, for our lamps are going out," but the wise replied, "There will not be enough for us and for you; go instead to the dealers and buy for yourselves."

But while they were going away to buy, the bridegroom came and those who were (prepared) went in with him to the marriage feast; and the door was shut. Later the other virgins also came and said, "Lord, Lord, open (the door) to us." But He replied, "I solemnly declare unto you, I do not know you (I am not acquainted with you." [Matt. 25:1-12 AMP]

We are living in the most exciting times since the book of Acts and, simultaneously, the most dangerous times ever known to mankind. The signs pointing to the return of the Lord are everywhere. We are nearing the end of the present Age of Grace, and many of God's people are excited about this reality and are making preparations for the Lord's return with great enthusiasm.

However, there are many that name Jesus as Lord who are not ready, and the time to get ready is extremely short. Jesus said, "Not everyone that saith unto me, Lord, Lord, shall enter into the kingdom of heaven; but he that doeth the will of my Father, which is in heaven" [Matt. 6:21].

Jesus also said, "Many will say unto me in that day, Lord, Lord, have we not prophesied in thy name? And in thy name have cast out devils? And in thy name done many wonderful works?" Works alone aren't what the Lord is looking for. Jesus specifically said that he that does the will of the Father would be granted access into the kingdom of heaven.

Some are under the impression that they are somehow in right relationship with God based off of their outward works for Him, because they've done good works or are in ministries that meet the needs of people, and they are going to be shocked. Works and acts of kindness aren't going to carry much weight in the day of the Lord if there hasn't been an intimate relationship with the Lord. Jesus isn't very interested in the works that we accomplish in our own strength, ability, or might. For two thousand years, God has been looking for one thing: relationship. Jesus said that the Father is looking for worshipers that will worship Him in spirit and truth. Works alone aren't the root to inclusion in the glorious Rapture of the Church; its **relationship, obedience,** and **love.**

Notice what Jesus said in Matthew 6:23: "And then will I profess unto them, I never knew you, depart from me ye that work iniquity." It's amazing to me that some of those doing the works of God are actually living in iniquity. They look pretty good on the outside; however, they only had a form of godliness and denied the power thereof [2 Tim. 3:5]. They were one thing out in the open and another behind closed doors.

Not only must we be ready for the Rapture, which is about to occur, but we must also be prepared to give an account to God for the life we've lived on the earth [1 Cor. 3:1-15]. In the scripture above pertaining to the ten virgins, Jesus was describing two groups of people who were scheduled to meet the bridegroom. One group was prepared, while the other group wasn't.

The bridegroom in this parable is a depiction of Jesus Christ. Jesus called all ten of these individuals virgins. In this verse of Scripture, the word "virgin" denotes purity of the Christian doctrine and character, so we can say that they were pure in heart and called to meet the bridegroom when He appeared. God desires that every believer walk in purity and uprightness of heart. I personally believe that the five virgins who were foolish once had hearts that burned for God but became cold, indifferent, and backslidden, without returning to the Lord to make things right.

Jesus made a powerful statement regarding looking back in the gospel of Luke. "No man having put his hand to the plough, and looking back, is fit for the kingdom of God" [Luke 9:62]. Here Jesus points out that the one who looks back isn't ready for the kingdom of God. Much can be gleaned from the awesome parable of the ten virgins, which, in my opinion, depicts the condition of the end-time Church right before the coming of the Lord. In verse eight, the unprepared virgins ask the wise virgins for some of their oil, but that request isn't granted because neither they nor we in this present generation can give away our oil, which represents the anointing and a relationship with God. Each believer has his or her own responsibility to develop and cultivate a relationship with the Lord through the Holy Spirit.

We must not allow ourselves to become like the foolish virgins in the parable who weren't ready and became complacent and lazy. Even though they knew that the bridegroom could appear at any moment, they failed to prepare for that day. Jesus said to "watch therefore: for ye know not what hour your Lord doth come" [Matt. 24:42]. Peter also warned about watching and being sober when he wrote, "But the end of all things is at hand: be ye therefore sober, and watch unto prayer" [1 Pet. 4:7]. Christians that are asleep are out of fellowship with the Lord and are presently living in a backslidden condition.

> And that, knowing that now it is high time to awake out of sleep for now is our salvation nearer than when believed. The night is far spent, the day is at hand: let us therefore cast off the works of darkness and let us put on the armour of light. [Rom. 13:11-12]

> Awake to righteousness, and sin not: for some have
> not the knowledge of God: I speak this to your
> shame. [1 Cor. 15:34 KJV]

What's also very interesting to me is that although the five foolish virgins had knowledge that the time of the bridegroom was near, they still didn't have enough sense to think ahead to plan for their trip. They knew the custom—they knew that if the call went forth, it could come at daybreak or midnight, and that preparation was a must, but they, like many of us in the Church today, were too occupied with other things.

The Amplified Bible refers to the five foolish virgins as thoughtless and without forethought. The other five are referred to as wise, sensible, intelligent, and prudent. We would say that they are on fire for God and looking unto the coming of the Lord at any moment.

How would God classify you in your walk with Him? Would you be among the Christians who are wise, sensible, intelligent, and prudent with an ongoing relationship with God? Or would you be among those who are foolish, thoughtless, and without forethought with regard to their relationship with the Lord?

We must judge ourselves today and make the necessary adjustments to our Christian walk so that we will not be without oil, the presence of God, in this last hour. The wise virgins were not willing to jeopardize their place at the marriage feast with the bridegroom for those who didn't prepare. They paid a price for what they had, and they only had enough for themselves. They were smart and didn't allow the influence of those that were not prepared to move them into complacency.

It's impossible to really know the Lord intimately through someone else. Association with anointed people will add to our lives, but association alone isn't enough. We must know Christ for ourselves. This is the reason the Lord sent us His blessed Holy Spirit. The Holy Spirit is the person who was sent in Christ's place to be with us and teach us all things.

> Howbeit when he, the Spirit of truth is come, he will guide you into all truth: for he shall not speak of himself: but whatsoever he shall hear that shall he speak: and he will shew you things to come. He shall glorify me: for he shall receive of mine, and shall shew it unto you. [John 16:13-14 KJV]

If we follow the leadership of the Holy Ghost, He will see to it that we are where we need to be in Christ when the trump of God sounds. The Holy Ghost is the one who will keep us focused on Christ, and as long as we so desire, He will keep us walking on that straight and narrow path that leads to life eternal. Jesus said that it was expedient that He leave the earth so that the Holy Spirit could come and be a comforter to us [John 16:7].

The five foolish virgins did not take the time to prepare to meet their Lord. They were probably too busy with the things of this life to think about bringing extra oil to light their candlesticks for the journey. They were completely unprepared and thought that they could get some oil from the wise virgins. This is probably one of the reasons why the Bible calls them foolish virgins.

They didn't think it was necessary to bring an extra supply of oil for their lamps. This is the mistake that some of us make today. I have heard people say that they would start a relationship with God when they are ready, and until that time comes, to just leave them be. They waste years and years running and don't take into account that a relationship is not built overnight, nor in a moment; it's a process of time.

The foolish virgins didn't discern the times in which they were living; they had no clue that the time of the bridegroom was near. They did not have a desire to see the bridegroom, for if they were prepared to meet him, they would have made sure that they had what it took to make the journey, instead of relying on others. Depending on the anointing of someone else isn't what will get us through; we must individually have that anointing upon our lives.

Jesus paid a heavy price for the anointing to come upon us. The only way to have that abiding presence of God in you and upon you is by faith in the Lord Jesus Christ; He is the one who anoints. This anointing isn't free; it's going to cost us something, and to be frank with you, it's going to cost you and I everything.

Jesus said that if we desire to follow Him, we must take up our cross daily, which means continually saying no to the desires of the flesh and yes to the Spirit. Paul the apostle admonished us when he wrote:

> For they that are after the flesh do mind the things of the flesh: but they that are after the spirit the things of the spirit. For to be carnally minded is death: but to be spiritually minded is life and peace. Because the carnal mind is enmity against God: for it is not

subject to the law of God, neither indeed can be. So then they that are in the flesh cannot please God. [Rom. 8:5-7]

Only those led by the Spirit of God have abiding within them the oil of gladness that brings insight, strength, and wisdom. The key that's missing in the lives of so many people of God is the leading of the Holy Spirit. When we allow the Spirit of God to work His work within us, we will find victory for every failure.

For if ye live after the flesh, ye shall die: but if ye through the Spirit do mortify the deeds of the body, ye shall live. For as many as are led by the Spirit of God, they are the sons of God. [Rom. 8:13-14]

I believe that the five wise virgins had more of a love for the bridegroom than the five foolish virgins. And because of their diligence and preparation, they were ready and had what they needed in the midnight hour to finish their course and meet the bridegroom without spot or wrinkle. The Word of God was a lamp unto their feet and a light unto their path.

On the other hand, the foolish virgins had no direction or clarity. They were in darkness after their lamps went out. Do you have enough oil as we approach midnight? Once Jesus comes and raptures the Church out of the earth, there won't be enough time to prepare. It will be too late, and you will be left unprepared, just like the foolish virgins were, if you do not bring enough oil for your journey. This is why Jesus told us to be ready at all times.

Watch, therefore and give strict attention, be cautious and active, for you do not know in what kind of a day your Lord is coming. But understand this: that had the householder known in what part of the night, whether in a night or a morning watch the thief was coming, he would have watched and would not have allowed his house to be undermined and broken through. You also must be ready therefore; for the Son of Man is coming at an hour when you do not expect Him.

Who then is the faithful, thoughtful and wise servant, whom his master has put in charge of his household, to give to the others the food and supplies at the proper time? Blessed, happy and fortunate and to be envied is that servant whom when his master comes he will find so doing. I solemnly declare to you, he will set him over all his possessions. But if that servant is wicked and says to himself, my master is delayed and is going to be gone a long time, and begins to beat his fellow servants, and to eat and drink with the drunken, the master of that servant will come on a day when he does not expect him and at and hour of which he is not aware, and will punish him, cut him up by scourging and put him with the pretenders (hypocrites); there will be weeping and grinding of teeth. [Matt. 24:42-51 AMP]

We must spend quality time with God, which will bring us into a deeper relationship of intimacy with Him, which will then bring the anointing on our lives.

Note: When the bridegroom finally came, he told the five foolish virgins who went to purchase more oil to complete their journey, "Verily I say unto you, I know you not" [Matt. 25:12].

Those are the saddest four words in the entire Bible, and unfortunately, many will hear those very words from the Lord. He's either Lord of all, or He isn't Lord at all. He wants first place in our life and will not share that position with anyone or anything. If you have drifted backwards in your walk with the Lord, He's standing in the same place you left Him. He's willing to reestablish a relationship with you before it's too late.

The Word of God tells us that obedience is better than sacrifice [1 Sam. 15:22]. The bridegroom knew the wise virgins that had their full supply of oil. Jesus said that His sheep know His voice, and another voice they will not follow [John 10:4-5 KJV].

So we have learned that God requires much more of us than just attending church, hearing a good sermon, and then going home and doing absolutely nothing with the message that was preached. It's time that we not only talk about the power of God, but demonstrate that power, by walking with God through the reading of his word and daily meditation on his promises, if I had to sum it all up with one word, it would be relationship.

We must be doers of the Word and not hearers only [James 1:22 KJV]. Those that hear the Word but don't do what they have heard are only deceiving themselves. We can't jump in and out of our relationship with the Lord; we must trust Him and be consistent in this walk of faith.

We are living in very serious times. Prophecies are being fulfilled right before our eyes, and the coming of the Lord is getting closer and closer. Every day that passes brings us closer to the reality of His appearing to redeem His Church. Jesus promised that He would return in an unexpected hour, so let's be ready at all times. "Watch therefore for ye know not what hour your Lord doth come" [Matt. 24:42].

WHO WILL BE LEFT BEHIND?

*E*veryone who has trusted Jesus Christ as Lord and Savior is ready for His coming and will be "caught up" into heaven during the Rapture. That includes the deceased saints from all centuries, as well as believers who are living on the earth at that time. Believers around the world make up the universal Church, which is called the body of Christ.

> For the Lord himself shall descend from heaven with a shout, with the voice of the archangel, and with the trump of God: and the dead in Christ shall rise first: Then we which are alive and remain shall be caught up together with them in the clouds, to meet the Lord in the air: and so shall we ever be with the Lord. [1 Thess. 4:16-17]

Those who have not received Jesus Christ as their Lord and Savior will be left behind on earth. Unfortunately, the left behind will include believers who may have been churchgoers who only had a form of godliness but rejected the Lordship of Jesus Christ in their lives [2 Tim. 3:5].

At the time of the Rapture, those left behind will realize they were not prepared to meet the Lord and will have to endure the coming Tribulation Period that will last seven years [Matt. 24:50-51].

> Therefore be ye also ready: for in such an hour as ye think not the Son of man cometh. Who then is a faithful and wise servant, whom his lord hath made ruler over his household to give them meat in due season? Bless is that servant, whom his lord when he cometh shall find so doing. Verily I say unto you, that he shall make him ruler over all his goods. [Matt. 24:44-47 KJV]

> Not everyone that saith unto me, Lord, Lord shall enter into the kingdom of heaven; but he that doeth the will of my father, which is in heaven. Many will say to me in that day, Lord, Lord have we not prophesied in they name? And in thy name have cast out devils? And in thy name done many wonderful works? And then will I profess unto them, I never knew you: depart from me ye that work iniquity. [Matt. 7:21-23 KJV]

Just as works didn't save us, works apart from grace won't get us into heaven. We are living in a time of great deception, not only in the world but also in the Church. Jesus isn't interested in how much we do in His name as much as He is in our obedience to His Word. Jesus wants to be the King and Lord of our lives, not just an escape from hell.

What a shock it will be for many on that day, when the Lord descends from heaven and takes His Church out of the earth. Millions will cry out in fear and unbelief as they awaken to the reality of being left behind. Many church people, including ministers of the gospel, will be left behind on that day.

Many pastors may be ministering at the time of the Rapture, when suddenly, without warning, the trump of God will sound and the dead in Christ will rise; then those that are alive and ready will be taken up into heaven in the twinkling of an eye [1 Thess. 4:16].

For those who played games with their salvation when the Church was upon the earth, this will be a time of great sorrow and regret.

Immediately after the Rapture, things on earth will dramatically change. The world will be faced with dangers it has not seen in all of history. There will be panic and fear everywhere as millions of people disappear from the earth.

ARE YOU PREPARED?

In his writings, the apostle Peter admonished us that the Lord is not slack concerning His promises as pertaining to His coming and the judgment of the nations. "But that God is longsuffering toward us, not willing that any should perish, but that all should come to repentance" [2 Pet. 3:7-9].

The Bible warns that there will be people that say in their heart that the Lord isn't really coming, and they will begin to live carnally. Those that try to put off the coming of the Lord and not prepare, even after seeing the signs of the times, could very likely become evil in heart and go back to the worldly way of living.

Many of God's people are living in bondage and defeat because they aren't looking to the coming of the Lord; they also lack the fear of God.

But and if that evil servant shall say in his heart, My lord delayeth his coming; and shall begin to smite his fellow servants, and to eat and drink with the drunken; the lord of that servant shall come in a day

when he looketh not for him, and in an hour that he
is not aware of. [Matt. 24:48-50 KJV]

Looking for the coming of the Lord will inspire us that believe to get on fire for Christ and finish the work to which He has called all of us, which is to preach the gospel to every creature. The knowledge of the Lord's coming should affect the way we give our money in supporting the work of God around the world and change the very way we think about life. Our compassion for those who aren't in fellowship with the Lord will greatly intensify; those that await the coming of the Lord are some of the greatest soul winners alive today.

THE PURPOSE OF THE RAPTURE

*T*he purpose of the Rapture is to take the Church of Jesus Christ out of the world in order to escape the Great Tribulation. The Rapture is the blessed hope for the believers who have received Christ before God judges the world. To fully understand the purpose of the Rapture and the events that will follow, you must understand the following prophetic word that God gave to the Old Testament prophet Daniel:

> Seventy weeks are determined upon thy people and upon thy holy city, to finish the transgression, and to make an end of sins, and to make reconciliation for iniquity, and to bring in everlasting righteousness, and to seal up the vision and prophecy, and to anoint the most Holy. Know therefore and understand, that from the going forth of the commandment to restore and to build Jerusalem unto the Messiah the Prince shall be seven weeks, and threescore and two weeks: the street shall be built again, and the wall, even in troublous times.

And after threescore and two weeks shall Messiah
be cut off, but not for himself: and the people of
the prince that shall come shall destroy the city and
the sanctuary; and the end thereof shall be with a
flood, and unto the end of the war desolations are
determined. And he shall confirm the covenant with
many for one week: and in the midst of the week he
shall cause the sacrifice and the oblation to cease,
and for the overspreading of abominations he shall
make it desolate, even until the consummation, and
that determined shall be poured upon the desolate.
[Dan. 9:24-27 KJV]

There are at least fourteen parts to this prophecy, and without
a proper understanding of them, you can't fully understand many
other prophecies. The meaning of the seventy weeks literally means
seventy, seventy weeks of 7 as in 70x7 which equals out to 490
years. The Hebrew word for week is "shabua," which means seven.

This vision given to Daniel doesn't concern days, but years.
The seventy weeks are divided into three separate events.

The first seven prophetic weeks of years total up to forty-nine
years, as 7x7=49. The second sixty-two prophetic weeks of years
total up to 434 years, as 62x7=434. The third week of years totals
up to seven years, which combined are a total of 490 years. The
seventy prophetic weeks of years began with the commandment
to restore and build Jerusalem. There were actually three decrees
given for the restoration of Jerusalem. The first decree was given
in the first year of King Cyrus of Persia [Ezra 1:1-5].

The second decree was given by Darius the Mede, in the second year of his reign. Darius reactivated the decree of Cyrus, and the temple was completed; but the city of Jerusalem had not yet been restored. Artaxerxes gave the third and final decree in 445 BC; at this time, Nehemiah rebuilt the walls of Jerusalem, which had fallen.

The calculation of the 490 weeks of years from the time the decree to rebuild Jerusalem was issued to Nehemiah in 445 BC is recorded in Nehemiah 2:1-9. Nehemiah was stirred to fast and pray after hearing that the walls of Jerusalem were burned down and was very saddened in his heart. Then King Artaxerxes asked, "Why is thy countenance sad, seeing thou art not sick? This is nothing else but sorrow of heart" [Neh. 2:2].

Nehemiah then asked the king if he pleased the king and if he had found favor in the king's sight to allow him to go to Judah, unto the city of his father's sepulchers, that he may rebuild it [Neh. 2:5]. The king permitted Nehemiah to go and gave him a letter to give to the governor of Jerusalem allowing him safe passage and another letter permitting him to receive timber to rebuild the walls.

This took place in the twentieth year of Artaxerxes. History tells us that the date of Artaxerxes's ascension to the throne of Persia was 465 BC. The twentieth year of his reign would place the date of this decree at 445 BC. We now have the beginning of the prophecy God gave to Daniel of the seventy weeks of years.

> Know therefore and understand, that from the going
> forth of the commandment to restore and to build
> Jerusalem unto the Messiah the Prince shall be
> seven weeks, and threescore and two weeks, the

street shall be build again, and the wall, even in troublous times. [Dan. 9:25]

In this verse, the angel of the Lord told Daniel to "know and understand" the events that were about to happen.

Daniel had an understanding of Jeremiah's prophecy of the seventy years of captivity for the Jewish people in Babylon. This is what caused Daniel to seek his God, since he wanted to know what God's plan for Israel was when the captivity of seventy years was over [Dan. 9:2-3].

The angel of the Lord told Daniel that Israel's restoration wouldn't be complete until seventy weeks of years had passed. The word "week" is translated from a Hebrew word meaning years.

The seven weeks, forty-nine years, ended when Jerusalem was rebuilt. The following sixty-two weeks are 434 years, which are commonly known as the silent years. This is the period between the Old Testament and the time leading up to Christ's death on the cross. The crucifixion put a temporary halt in God's timeline for the Jews and began the age in which we presently live, called the Church Age, or the Age of Grace.

This age is like a parenthesis in the seventy weeks of Daniel. The Rapture of the Church will signal the end of the Church Age and will then resume the seventy weeks of years.

Now, let's review the key points of this prophecy. The seventy weeks of years are divided into three sections: the first seven weeks of years, 7x7=49 years; the second sixty-two weeks, 62x7=434 years; and the third week are a total of seven years.

The first two have already been fulfilled. Dating from 445 BC, the date that the decree to build Jerusalem was issued (Neh. 2:1-7),

to the entry of Christ Jesus into Jerusalem, five days before His crucifixion in AD 33, would be a total of 483 years. Note that Daniel
was told that a total of 490 years would complete the cycle.

We still have seven years left, which will begin when the
Anti-Christ signs a covenant of peace with the Jewish people
after the Rapture of the Church. This will be the beginning of the
Tribulation Period.

WHEN WILL THE RAPTURE TAKE PLACE?

The Bible says that the Rapture will occur suddenly, without any announcement. Peter compares it to a thief in the night [2 Pet. 3:10]. No one knows the exact timing of the Rapture of the Church, but signs indicate the season. It could happen at any moment. Many of the signs that Jesus gave us have already been fulfilled, and some are presently beginning to be fulfilled.

We are definitely seeing more signs now than any other generation since the birth of Christ. It's clear from Scripture that the Rapture will take place before the Tribulation Period begins. Paul says, "For God hath not appointed us to wrath, but to obtain salvation by our Lord Jesus Christ" [1 Thess. 5:9 KJV].

Let's take a look at what the apostle John wrote concerning the Rapture.

> After this I looked, and, behold, a door was opened
> in heaven: and the first voice which I heard was as
> it were of a trumpet talking with me; which said,
> come up hither, and I will show thee things which
> must be hereafter. [Rev. 4:1 KJV]

The first two words of this verse, "after this," are derived from the Greek phrase meta-tauta, which means is after the things, which concern the churches, or after the dispensation of grace has ended. I believe that the Bible is clear here and that the Rapture will take place before the Tribulation begins. There are many reasons for believing that the Rapture will precede the seven-year Tribulation Period, as outlined in the book of Revelation. Jesus is quoted in the book of Luke as saying that we should be prepared to escape to stand before the Son of Man.

> And take heed to yourselves, lest at anytime your hearts be overcharged with surfeiting, and drunkenness, and cares of this life, and so that day come upon you unawares. For as a snare shall it come on all them that dwell on the face of the whole earth. Watch ye therefore, and pray always, that ye may be accounted worthy to escape all these things that shall come to pass, and to stand before the Son of man. [Luke 21:34-36 KJV]

The people to whom Jesus is referring that will be worthy to escape are born-again believers. Paul also admonished the Church regarding the coming of Christ, declaring,

> And now ye know what with holdeth that he might be revealed in his time. For the mystery of iniquity doth already work: only he who now letteth will let, until he be taken out of the way. And then shall that Wicked be revealed, whom the Lord shall consume

with the spirit of his mouth, and shall destroy with
the brightness of his coming. [2 Thess. 2:6-8 KJV]

The word "he" in verse seven is referring to the Church, the
Body of Christ. Some believers are of the opinion that the "he" here
is referring to the Holy Spirit, but if the Holy Spirit were taken out
of the earth during this time, no one could be saved. And the Bible
is clear that after the Rapture of the Church, there will be a move
of God in the earth, and many will be saved.

Some within the Church believe that the Church of Jesus Christ
will go through the Tribulation Period, while others believe that
the Church will only experience a part of it. I believe that both of
these doctrines are in error, and I would like for everyone reading
this book not to take my word for it, but to study it on your own so
that you won't have any question regarding when the church will
leave earth. God wants you to know!

There are many scriptures in the Bible that support the pre-Tribulation view point, but one that stands out the most for me is
Revelation 4:1, in which the Church is seen in heaven, where it
will be with Jesus until the seven years of Tribulation are over.
Revelation chapters 1-3 represent the Church on earth in what
is called the Church Age, or the Age of Grace. After Revelation
chapter 3, the Church is only seen in heaven.

Those that teach that there won't be any Rapture are in effect
misleading people and causing them not to look for what the Bible
calls the blessed hope. The Bible declares that Jesus will come
back for those that are looking for Him, giving the impression that
if you're not looking, you may not be going.

So Christ was once offered to bear the sins of many;
and unto them that look for Him shall he appear the
second time without sin unto salvation. [Heb. 9:28]

It is my prayer that this book will help provide an understanding
on this very important topic, dispel myths and misunderstandings,
and remove the complexity of a subject that God wants His people
to be knowledgeable about.

PEACE AND SAFETY

But as to the suitable times and the precise seasons
and dates, brethren, you have no necessity for anything being written to you, for you yourselves know
perfectly well that the day of the (return of the) Lord
will come (as unexpectedly and suddenly) as a thief
in the night. When people are saying, all is well
and secure, and, there is peace and safety, then in
a moment unforeseen destruction (ruin and death)
will come upon them as suddenly as labor pains
come upon a woman with child; and they shall
by no means escape, for there will be no escape.
[1 Thess. 5:1-3 AMP]

As the world witnessed the 1993 Oslo agreement being signed
on the lawn of the White House between Palestinian Liberation
Organization (PLO) Chairman Yasser Arafat and the former prime
minister of Israel Yitzhak Rabin, I'm sure that everyone watching
thought peace would finally come to the Middle East. However,
since that day until our present, the fighting has continued, and
things have deteriorated to such a degree that an all-out war in the
region could be imminent.

Real peace will not be fully realized until the Prince of Peace, Jesus Christ, the Son of God, returns to the earth. I appreciate the United States and her western allies for attempting to bring peace to this area of the world, but the problems in the Middle East go back several thousands of years; only the coming of the Messiah can bring a closure to this conflict once and for all.

As we witness the end-time prophecies of the Bible being fulfilled with breathtaking speed and biblical accuracy, we should also know that the coming of a one-world dictator with a one-world agenda is on the horizon and that Israel's darkest days are yet to come.

Their greatest days, however, will be coming shortly thereafter. The Church must be very careful in how it deals with the nation of Israel. In certain Christian circles, there are some who teach that the Church has replaced Israel and that the blessings that once belonged to Israel now belong to the Church. I believe that this is a dangerous, unscriptural teaching that cannot be supported by Scripture. The Church hasn't replaced Israel, and it never will. According to Galatians, the Church of Jesus Christ is an extension of the Jewish nation.

> Know and understand that it is really the people
> who live by faith who are the true sons of Abraham.
> And the scripture, foreseeing that God would jus-
> tify, declare righteous, put in right standing with
> Himself, the Gentiles in consequence of faith, pro-
> claimed the Gospel foretelling the glad tidings of a
> Savior long beforehand to Abraham in the promise,
> saying that in you shall all the nations of the earth

be blessed. So then, those who are people of faith
are blessed and made happy and favored by God
as partners in fellowship with the believing and
trusting Abraham. [Gal. 3:7-9 AMP]

And if ye be Christ's, then are ye Abraham's seed,
and heir's according to the promise. [Gal. 3:29 AMP]

Here we see that everyone who trusts Jesus Christ as Savior and
Lord are one with Abraham by faith. To believe that the Church
has replaced Israel is completely wrong. The Jewish people have
a destiny in God that will be fulfilled, and nothing on earth will
be able to alter that plan because it has been written in the eternal
Word of God. God's plan for the Jewish people will be fulfilled,
and one day in the future, Jesus Christ Himself will rule the world
from Jerusalem.

And it shall come to pass, that every one that is left of
all the nations which came against Jerusalem shall
even go up from year to year to worship the King,
the Lord of hosts, and to keep the feast of taberna-
cles. And it shall be, that whosoever will not come
up of all the families of the earth unto Jerusalem to
worship the King, the Lord of host, even upon them
shall be no rain. [Zech. 14:16-17 KJV]

ISRAEL STANDS ALONE

Behold, the day of the Lord cometh, and thy spoil
shall be divided in the midst of thee. For I will
gather all nations against Jerusalem to battle; and
the city shall be taken, and the houses rifled, and the
women ravished; and half of the city shall go forth
into captivity, and the residue of the people shall not
be cut off from the city. [Zech. 14:1-2 KJV]

*I*n the very near future, a horrible time is coming when Israel, the
beloved people of God, will stand alone in a world of hostile
enemies that desire nothing more than her complete destruction. In
1922, the United Nations gave Britain responsibility over Palestine
to bring about the intent of the Balfour Declaration, which called
for a homeland to be created for the Jewish people. It was origi-
nally a trusteeship, but Britain gave nearly 70 percent of the land
to King Abdullah of Jordan.

A Jewish presence was established in 1947, when the United
Nations established the Partition of Palestine, with the hope of
internationalizing Jerusalem. But the Arabs, not desiring a Jewish

State in Israel, rejected the plan. Israel, however, accepted the plan and declared that they were a Jewish State on May 14, 1948.

> Therefore, behold, the days come, saith the Lord, that it shall no more be said, The Lord liveth, that brought up the children of Israel out of the land of Egypt; But, the Lord liveth, that brought up the children of Israel from the land of the north, and from all the lands whither he had driven them: and I will bring them again into their land that I gave unto their fathers. Behold, I will send for many fishers, saith the Lord, and they shall fish them; and after will I send for many hunters, and they shall hunt them from every mountain, and from every hill, and out of the holes of the rocks. [Jer. 16:14-15]

Immediately after Israel became a nation, seven Arab States attacked Israel. The United States of America didn't allow arm shipments to come into the country, forcing Israel to turn to the former Soviet Union for weapons and supplies. In 1948, Jordan illegally took Judea, Samaria, and Jerusalem, while Egypt took the Gaza Strip.

From 1948 to 1967, Jordan and Egypt moved into these areas without a single word of protest from the rest of the world, including the United Nations. During this time, there was not even a word of establishing a so-called Palestinian State. In 1949, against all hope, Israel pushed back the invading armies, then other countries stepped in and called for a cease-fire.

It's amazing to me that other Arab leaders have not offered the Palestinians a homeland anywhere else in the Middle East, but have chosen to fight for Jerusalem, which isn't even bigger than the state of New Jersey. During the Six-Day War in 1967, five Arab States attacked Israel again, but with the help of the Lord, Israel defended herself and came out victorious once again. Israel was able to recapture and secure all of Samaria, Jerusalem, and the Gaza Strip, land given to them by God.

> In the same day the Lord made a covenant with Abram, saying, Unto they seed have I given this land, from the river of Egypt unto the great river, the river Euphrates: The Kenites, and the Kenizzites, and the Kadmonites, and the Hittites and the Perizzites, and the Rephaims, and the Amorites, and the Canaanites, and the Girgashites, and the Jebusites. [Gen. 15:18-21 KJV]

Today, Israel has only about one third of the land God promised to give them. However, when Jesus returns to the earth with His Church, He will establish His kingdom upon this very planet, and then Israel will be fully restored and be given all of the Land promise to them by God.

WORLD WAR III

In the future, the conflict between the Arabs and the Jewish people will climax to a point that will lead the world into its third world war. Many world leaders and politicians have tried to resolve this conflict with political tactics and promises. Peace agreements have been made but broken because the real problem can't be resolved by natural reasoning.

Although our world leaders are presently putting forth much effort in attempting to bring peace to the Middle East, none of them will be able to bring closure to this conflict, for it is not a political problem nor a social one, but a spiritual problem that only the Lord Jesus Christ can resolve.

This region is more dangerous now than ever before, and the stakes are very high. For years, both sides have hit one another with deadly force, and even though some progress has been made, time is surely running out.

In his writings, the prophet Ezekiel gave explicit details concerning what the world is about to see take place in the Middle East. God visited Ezekiel and told him to prophesy concerning this.

> And the word of the Lord came to me, saying, Son
> of man, set your face against Gog, of the land of

Magog, the chief prince of Meshech and Tubal, and prophesy against him, and say, Thus saith the Lord God: Behold, I am against thee, O Gog, the chief prince of Meshech and of Tubal: And I will turn thee back, and put hooks into thy jaws, and I will bring thee forth, and all thine army, horses and horsemen, all of them clothed with all sorts of armor, even great company with bucklers and shields, all of them handling swords: Persia, Ethiopia, and Libya with them; all of them with shield and helmet: Gomer, and all his bands; the house of Togarmah of the north quarters, and all his bands: and many people with thee. You (Gog) be prepared; yes prepare yourself, you and all your companies that are assembled about you, and you be a guard and a commander for them. After many days you shall be visited and mustered (for service); in the latter years you shall go against the land that is restored from the ravages of the sword, where people are gathered out of many nations upon the mountains of Israel, which had been a continual waste; but its (people) are brought forth out of the nations and they shall dwell securely, all of them. You shall ascend and come like a storm; you shall be like a cloud to cover the land, you and all your hosts and many people with you. Thus says the Lord God: At the same time thoughts shall come into your mind, and you will devise an evil plan. And you will say, I will go up against an open country, the land of unwalled villages; I will fall upon those who are at rest, who dwell securely, all of them dwelling without walls and having neither bars nor gates, to take a spoil and prey; to turn your hand upon the desolate places now inhabited, and assail the people gathered out of the nations, who have obtained livestock and goods, who dwell at the center of the earth Palestine. [Ezek. 38:1-12 AMP]

Here the prophet Ezekiel is giving us a detailed explanation of exactly what will take place in this war, which I believe will be World War III. Many teachers of Bible prophecy agree that the nations involved will be Russia, Germany, Turkey, Iran, Ethiopia, and Libya [Ezek. 38:5-6 KJV].

The Bible indicates that these nations will strike at a time when Israel is experiencing peace, dwelling safely in their own land.

After this war has ended, I believe that the Anti-Christ, the man of sin, will appear and attempt to bring about a peace agreement for seven years with the Arab world and the Jewish people and start what is called the seven-year Tribulation Period.

THE SEVEN-YEAR PEACE TREATY

> And he shall confirm the covenant with many for one week: and in the midst of the week he shall cause the sacrifice and the oblation to cease, and for the overspreading of abominations he shall make it desolate, even until the consummation, and that determined shall be poured upon the desolate. [Dan. 9:27 KJV]

Following the Rapture of the Church, Israel will enter into a covenant of peace with the Anti-Christ, who will come from the eastern division of the revised Roman Empire. According to the prophet Daniel, this treaty will give the Anti-Christ great respect around the world that will cause governments to gladly give him more power and authority (Dan. 8:23-25). This treaty will be significant because the entire world has been seeking peace in the Middle East for centuries without success.

> And through his policy also he shall cause craft to prosper in his hand; and he shall magnify himself in his heart, and by peace shall destroy many: he shall

also stand up against the Prince of princes; but he
shall be broken without hand. [Dan. 8:2 KJV]

For seven years, the Anti-Christ will rule throughout the Middle East and a large portion of the world. Three and a half years after the signing of this agreement, he will break the covenant of peace and plunge the world into great bloodshed. The world will then see that it was a false peace, and as a result, great trouble will break forth upon the entire planet, better describe as the Great Tribulation.

This will be the most significant event in the middle of the first part of the Tribulation Period, which will last for a total of seven years, as it signals the beginning of the very end of time as we know it. After the treaty is broken, the true nature of the Anti-Christ will be seen, but for many, it will be too late.

This will be the time when some of the greatest disasters the world has ever witnessed in all of its history will occur. Jesus said that no flesh could endure this period and that everyone left on the planet after the Rapture would perish, if it weren't for the elect's sake.

And if those days had not been shortened, no human
being would endure and survive, but for the elect
(God's chosen ones) those days will be shortened.
[Matt. 24:22 AMP]

9